In a Family, Everyone Helps

Children's Family Life Books

Speedy Publishing LLC
40 E. Main St. #1156
Newark, DE 19711
www.speedypublishing.com

A family is a group consisting of parents and children living together in a household.

In some families, the mother takes care of the children and does the chores around the house while the father is mainly responsible to earn and provide for the family.

However, this does not mean that the father and the children should just leave all the chores for the mom to do, especially if the mother also has a job outside the house.

Helping together in doing things around the house can strengthen the family and teach everyone the principles of work and cooperation.

Since it has always been a challenge to encourage everyone to lend a hand, here are some ways to inspire everyone to help.

1. HAVE A PLAN.

Discuss with everyone in the family the goals to achieve and the steps to take to achieve them.

Discuss the basic things that need to be done daily, weekly, monthly, quarterly, and yearly.

Set times for everything so nobody feels overwhelmed, and so the family can feel good about getting a lot of things done together.

Mia

TO DO LIST	TO DO	DONE
Practice the violin	✓	
Clean your room	✓	
Pick up clothes	✓	
Read 30 minutes		✓
Homework	✓	
TV-time (30 min)	✓	
Walk the dog	✓	
Swimming		✓
Ballet	✓	

John

TO DO LIST	TO DO	DONE
Soccer	✓	
Computer for 30 min		✓
Puzzle games	✓	
TV-Time (30 min)		✓
Swimming	✓	
Feed dog	✓	
Homework	✓	
Clean room		✓

Mom

TO DO LIST	TO DO	DONE
Yoga	✓	
Pick up clothes	✓	
Package the lunches	✓	
Laundry		✓
Practice drawing	✓	
Cook favorite treat	✓	
Read 30 minutes		✓
Time for hobby	✓	
Wash the dishes	✓	
Gym		✓
Farmer's Market		✓
Cleaning	✓	

Dad

TO DO LIST	TO DO	DONE
Run for 30 minutes	✓	
Drive kids to school	✓	
Lawn		✓
Special Projects		✓
Take the garbage out	✓	
Go to the zoo with kids	✓	
Take a trip with family	✓	
Walk/feed dog	✓	
Time for hobby		✓
Car service		✓
Golf	✓	
Boss BBQ		✓

2. ASSIGN TASKS APPROPRIATE TO EACH PERSON'S AGE AND PHYSICAL CAPABILITIES.

Consider what each member of the family can do according to their age, their physical capabilities, and what each loves to do.

When we acknowledge what a person wants to do, that person usually is inspired to fulfill that role.

TO DO LIST
Name Mia
Mo Tu We Th Fr Sa Su
Practice the violin
Clean your room
Pick up clothes
Read 30 minutes
Homework
TV-time (30min)
Walk the dog
Swimming
Ballet
To do list
Drive kids to school
Take out the garbge
Go to the zoo with kids
Walk/feed dog
Golf
Swimming

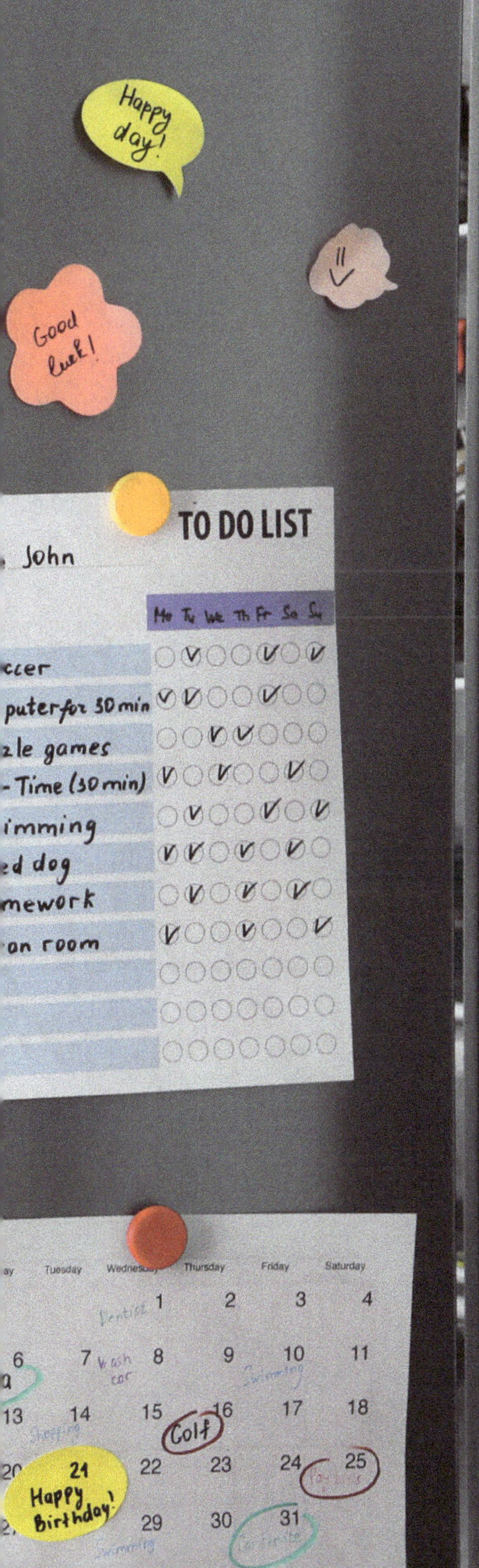

3. HAND OVER A LIST OF TASKS TO BE ACCOMPLISHED.

After you have determined the tasks that are appropriate for each individual, put a list of who does what on the door of the refrigerator,

or some other place where people will see it. That way nobody can "forget" which jobs are theirs.

To do list Mom
1. Exercise
2. Laundry
3. Carpool
4. Homework with kids
5. Time for hobby
6. Pack lunches
Things to Do!
Be Happy
To do list Dad
1. Run for 30 minutes
2. Drive kids to school
3. Prep for dinner
4. Go to the zoo with the kids
5. Take out the trash
6. Time for hobby
To do list Penelope
Make bed
4. Practice violin
5. Homework
6. Time for hobby
Have a nice day!
To do list Oliver
1. Make bed
2. Practice
3. Read 30 minutes
4. Time for hobby
5. Homework
Nice day!
This week

4. TEACH THEM HOW

The usual reason why some do not want to do something is that they find it hard to do and so they are hesitant to fulfill that task.

We usually get discouraged when we do things in a way that doesn't lead to good results.

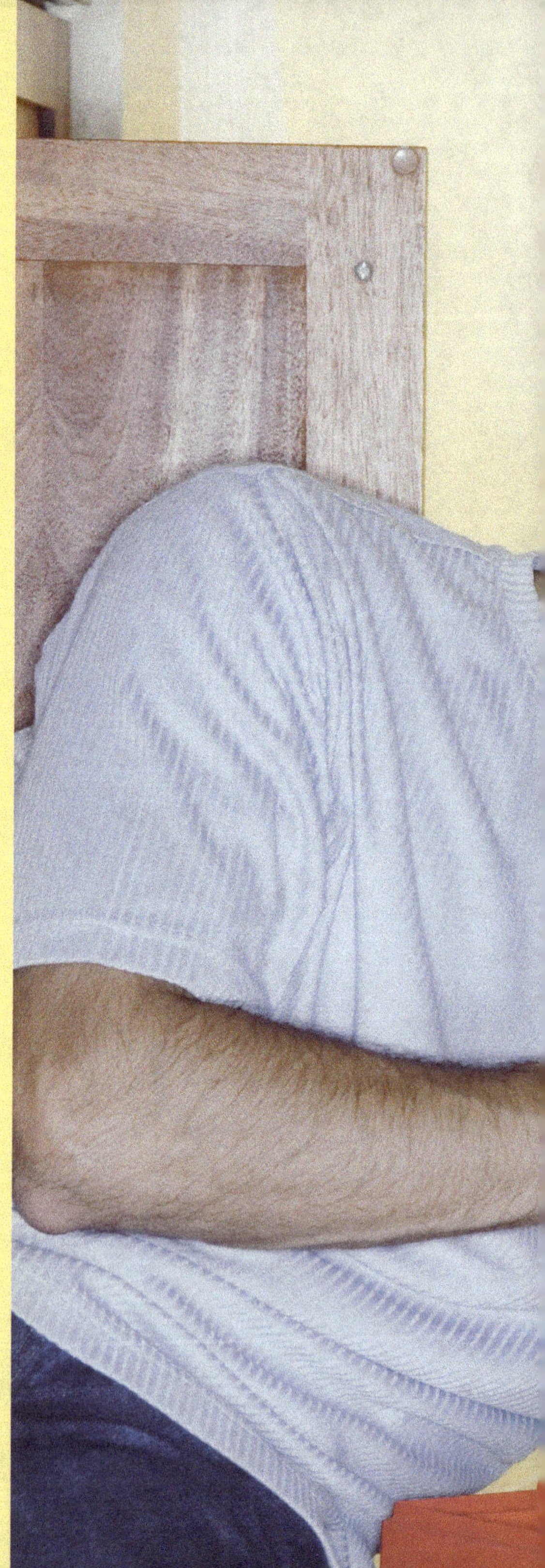

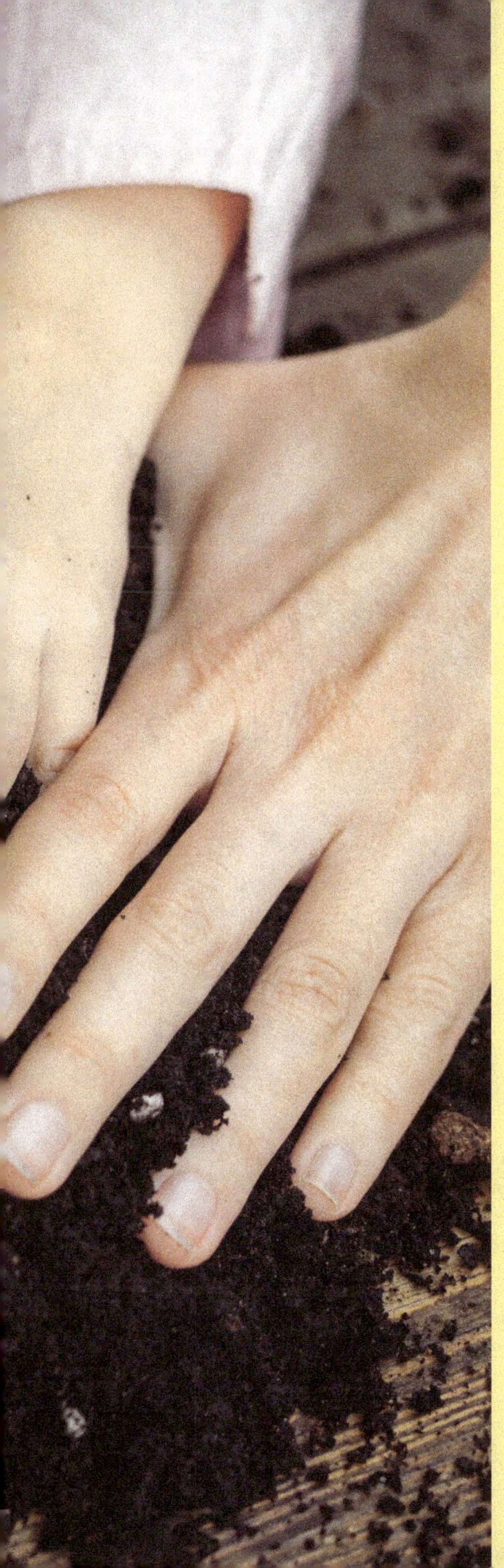

To give family members the courage to fulfill their tasks, take some time to teach them how to do those things.

Be patient, and show your appreciation for the progress they make.

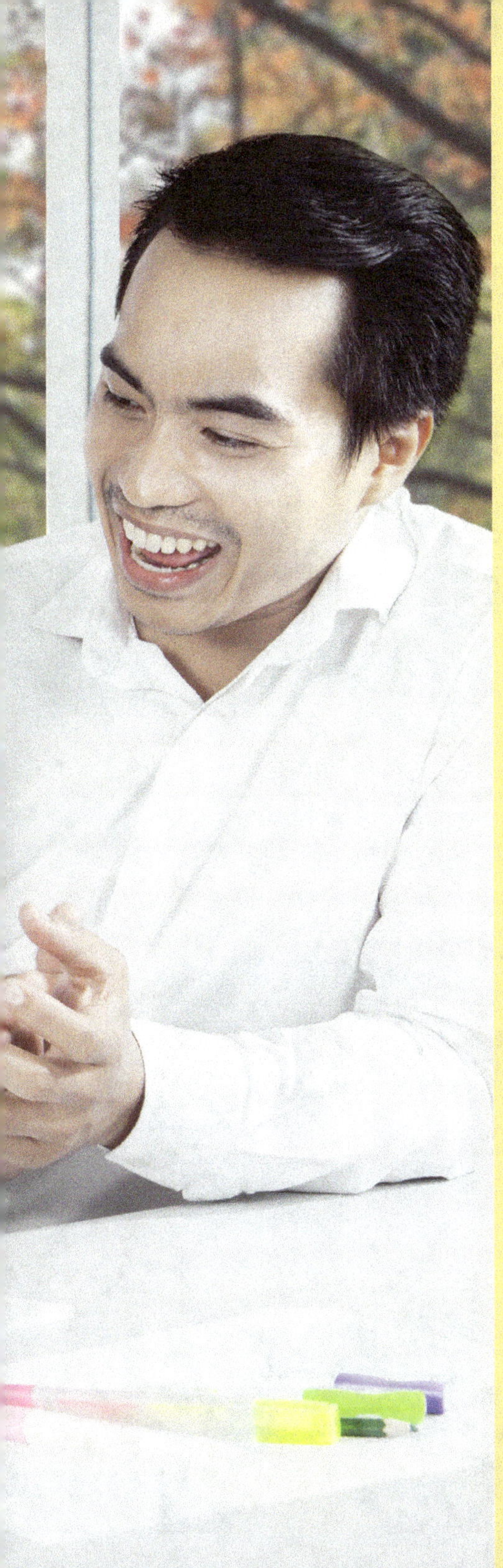

5. TREAT THE LITTLE HELPERS.

To encourage kids to help, give them some appreciation or even treat them with something that will make them smile.

These are just some ways to encourage every member of the family to help with the common task of keeping up with the chores around the house.

When everyone has a role to fulfill, everyone feels he or she belongs to the team and is an important part of the family.

www.ingramcontent.com/pod-product-compliance
Lightning Source LLC
LaVergne TN
LVHW060831170826
845678LV00010B/1953

* 9 7 9 8 8 6 9 4 4 4 0 9 7 *